ANDRE AGASSI

(Photo on front cover.)

Andre Agassi slams the ball at Pete Sampras during the French Open.

(Photo on previous pages.)

Agassi shows his championship cup to the center court fans at Wimbledon.

Photography supplied by Wide World Photos Inc.

Library of Congress Cataloging-in-Publication Data
Rambeck, Richard.
Andre Agassi / Richard Rambeck.
p. cm.
Summary: R elates how this tennis player won Grand
Slam events only after realizing that talent alone
was not enough and that he needed a new coach.
ISBN 1-56766-202-1 (lib. Bdg.)
1. Agassi, Andre. 1970- —Juvenile literature. 2.
Tennis players—United States—Biography—Juvenile
literature. [1. Agassi, Andre, 1970- 2. Tennis players.]
I. Title
GV994.A43R36 1995   95-6461
796.342'092 B—dc20   CIP
                                      AC

ANDRE
AGASSI

BY RICHARD RAMBECK

Andre Agassi walked slowly toward the court at Louis Armstrong Stadium in Flushing, New York. Agassi was about to play in the finals of the 1994 U.S. Open. His opponent was German star Michael Stich, but it didn't matter to Agassi who was on the other side of the net. He was determined to win. As fans chanted Agassi's name, he turned to talk to his coach, Brad Gilbert. "There's no way this guy's coming here and taking my title," Agassi said.

When the 1994 U.S. Open began, Andre Agassi wasn't expected to win more than one or two matches, let alone the tournament. Ranked 20th in world, he wasn't even one of the top 16 seeded players at the tournament. Agassi, who once was supposed to rise to the top of the game of tennis, was falling down the ladder. In 1988, he had been ranked third in the world. Six years later, he wasn't even the third best player in the U.S.

A gassi was only 18 years old in 1988. He had the natural ability to be as good as he wanted to be. "I've always had a gift," he said. "And my talent has gotten me through a lot of tough times." But talent wasn't enough. Agassi couldn't win the big tournaments, the Grand Slam

Agassi leaps in the air as he serves to his opponent.

*Agassi
returns a shot
from Thomas
Muster in the
1994 French
Open.*

events. The Grand Slam is made up of four tournaments — the Australian Open, the French Open, Wimbledon in England, and the U.S. Open.

Agassi made the finals of the French Open twice, but lost both times. He also lost in the finals of the 1990 U.S. Open, defeated by American Pete Sampras. In 1992, Agassi surprised the tennis world by winning Wimbledon. At the end of the final match, he fell to the court and cried. Now, the experts said, he would finally begin playing to the level of his ability. Even after his Wimbledon victory, however, Agassi didn't have much success.

In 1993, Agassi never came close to winning a big tournament. At the end of the year, he was ranked 24th in the world—the first time since 1987 he had not been in the top ten. "It was a nightmare," Agassi said of his play in 1993. Agassi knew he was wasting his talent. "Time's going by, and I'm not even on the path of figuring out what I need to do," Agassi said to his longtime friend, Perry Rogers.

But Agassi did figure out what to do. He hired Brad Gilbert as his new coach. Agassi admired Gilbert, also a professional tennis player. "He has spent his

Agassi defeats Goran Ivanisevic to win the 1992 Wimbledon men's singles champonship.

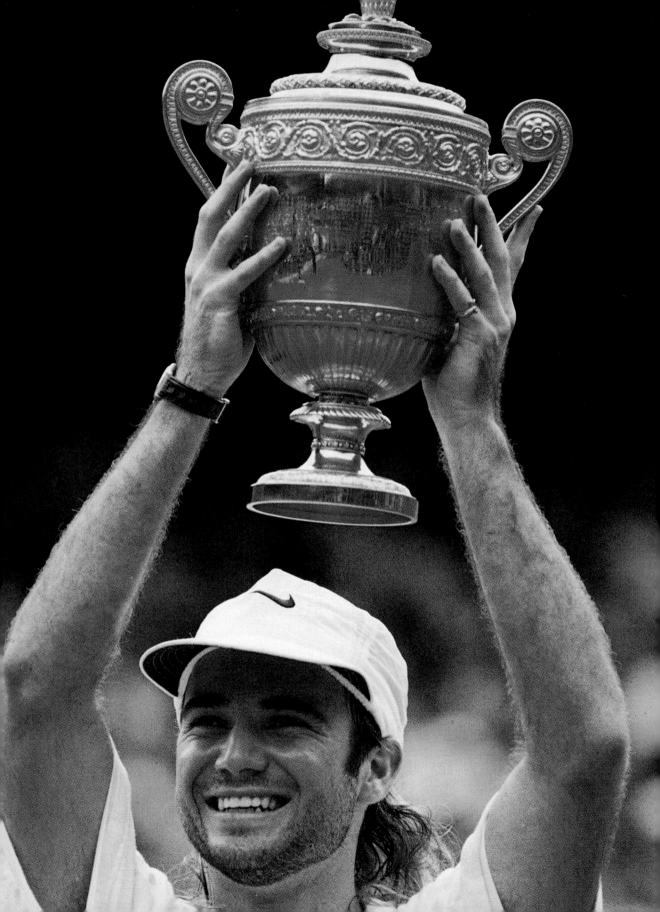

whole career winning matches he shouldn't have won," Agassi said of Gilbert. "I've done the opposite. I've lost a lot of matches I should not have lost." Gilbert taught Agassi how to think on the court, how to win the big points. Agassi proved to be a good student.

"I feel I should have won four or five Grand Slam titles by now, no question about that," Agassi said before the start of the 1994 U.S. Open. Nobody else knew it, but he was ready to play the best tournament of his life. Agassi reached the finals by beating four players ranked higher than he was. His toughest match was against

Michael Chang. Agassi beat Chang in a long, long five set match.

In the finals against Michael Stich, Agassi ran circles around the much taller German, winning the match in three sets, 6–1, 7–6, 7–5. After the winning point, Agassi fell to his knees on the court. The 20th ranked player in the world had won the U.S. Open! "Do you know what's been the greatest?" Gilbert said after Agassi won the title. "To see him become a great player, instead of just being a great hitter of the ball."

Agassi had won a Grand Slam event before, but this title was different.

He was a better player now, and he knew it. "When I won Wimbledon, it was a relief," Agassi said. "Winning this one, I feel I've made a surge forward. There's a difference between saying, 'Whew, I did it,' and saying, 'Yes, I can do it.'" After fighting himself for so many years, Agassi was finally ready to try to become the best.

Several weeks after winning the U.S. Open, Agassi captured the Paris Open championship. It was his fifth tournament victory of the year. In addition, the Paris Open title made Agassi the second ranked player in the world. Only Pete Sampras, who lost to Agassi in the Paris Open, was ahead of him. Agassi was ready to battle Sampras for the top ranking. "I certainly want to, and I certainly hope to," Agassi said.

S ampras already knew how tough an opponent Agassi could be. "He will be hard to beat for the next ten years," said Sampras. Before Agassi won the U.S. Open, Sampras had wished Agassi would again become one of the top players. Sampras got his wish. "The game needs him," Sampras said. "I think we have a

Agassi makes a return against Guy Forget during the 1991 Davis Cup Final.

20

rivalry that turns into something special because we kind of bring out the best in each other."

Andre Agassi realized something after winning the U.S. Open. "I can be the best player in the world," he said. He also realized he could be more than just the top player. Only 24 years old, he was now good enough to win several more Grand Slam events. "Hopefully, you can say, 'I was number one for a while,'" Agassi said. "But to win the Grand Slam tournaments is what is most important to me."